GLAMOUR GLOBALS
TRENDS OVER BRANDS

CREATED AND CONCEPTUALIZED BY SAID AGHIL BAAGHIL
WITH CO-AUTHORS MIRIAM MOSSALLI, YASMINE KHASHOGJI AND
ROLA ASHOUR ELABORATING ON THEIR RESPECTIVE FIELDS

iUniverse, Inc.
Bloomington

GLAMOUR GLOBALS
TRENDS OVER BRANDS

iUniverse books may be ordered through booksellers or by contacting:

iUniverse
1663 Liberty Drive
Bloomington, IN 47403
www.iuniverse.com
1-800-Authors (1-800-288-4677)

ISBN: 978-1-4759-7166-8 (sc)
ISBN: 978-1-4759-7167-5 (e)

Printed in the United States of America

iUniverse rev. date: 1/10/2013

TABLE OF CONTENTS

Part III: Yasmine Khashogji

Part IV: Rola Ashour

FOREWORD

WHY DO CERTAIN AUDIENCES TEND to be followers of trends and not brands? Is it the onset of sudden wealth and the need to be socially accepted? What role does self-esteem play in these tendencies? My co-authors and I have tried to look at all the angles and observe current consumer behavior in emerging markets to see why a certain group of people in which we're very interested, the Glamour Globals, might now be behaving differently toward brands, and preferring trends. We speak in general terms of several nations, but our primary focus is on emerging and frontier markets. I address the issue from a marketing perspective. My co-author Miriam Mosalli, a luxury consultant, then addresses the issue in more depth in the specific context of fashion. Another co-author, Yasmine Khashogji, a startup consultant, reveals some fascinating insight through a survey concerning our target audience's vacation preferences. Finally, co-author Rola Ashour, a psychologist, offers a way forward by suggesting ways that we might cultivate a better future for all through simple improvements in the way we treat one another, make decisions, and raise our children.

PART I:
SAID BAAGHIL

CHAPTER ONE:
INTRODUCTION

THE MODERN RICHE. THE BOURGEOISIE. The new money. The conspicuous consumer. The people we might call the "Glamour Globals." History, literature, and sociology unfortunately repeat the all-too-often sad tale of people who suddenly come into money, and seem to have no better purpose for that money than to flaunt it, needing ever more money so they can flaunt it ever more showily. And of course they desire to acquire ever more—more money, more belongings—and seemingly with no higher purpose than to show that they have these things. Money, for such people, is power and status, not to do something with, but to possess, end of story.

The story of people who were once poor suddenly coming into fantastic wealth is one we might predict would have a happy ending, fit for a fairy tale. And poor people coming into money is undoubtedly a good economic result for policymakers. But the story of new wealth as it unfolds in real life seldom seems to play out as it might if a Hollywood movie writer were scripting it.

If we sit and think about the old fairy tales which deal with new money a little more deeply, however, we might remember the wise warnings concerning sudden wealth that we see in many ancient stories—those of King Midas, the prodigal son, the blind Baba-Abdallah. We find that the perils—often deadly—of being newly rich are as old as humanity itself.

It must be said that it is not as though Old Money has ever

1

behaved terribly well—but perhaps our disappointment in today's New Money consumers is all the sharper because deep down inside we have such high hopes for poor people who now have access to wealth and the goods and power it can bring. Perhaps, we think, having seen the mistakes of past generations, this generation now coming into wealth will be the ones to get it right.

In taking a close look at human behavior as it relates to wealth, we may read the tale of "conspicuous consumption." Conspicuous consumption, a term from sociology, refers to people using buying decisions as a means of displaying their wealth and attaining social status. And we may even see the sad saga of conspicuous consumption's close cousin "invidious consumption"—which is the charming trait of displaying one's wealth through material possessions with the specific intention of invoking envy in others. These sad stories are replaying themselves again and again around the globe, as the globalized economy takes root in new regions and among people of all kinds who are experiencing modern wealth for the first time in their people's history.

Over the last several decades, starting first with the influx of natural wealth into once-impoverished nations in Asia and elsewhere, followed by the wealth now being brought to developing nations by virtue of the global economy, the rise of new wealth in the developing world has played out alongside the rise and then sudden collapse of the worldwide struggle between capitalism and communism. This reshifting left many third-world and developing nations with a void of homegrown entrepreneurial leadership, a discontinuity of values, and a general state of unrest and upheaval. This unhappy collision of (unequally) rising wealth and universally collapsing and shifting political and social structures has made today's version of the nouveau riche, the Glamour Globals, perhaps more vexing for marketers, sociologists and policymakers than any former manifestations of the newly rich. These rich people tend to be irrational consumers, consuming and choosing brands and products in a way that is not conducive to entrepreneurship and long-term prosperity in their home nations.

It might seem strange that a work written from a marketing perspective would express an interest in taming anyone's materialistic impulses, especially those of the people we generally serve, in the Middle East and Africa, the BRIC countries, and in Asia. The fact is, however, that it is in all of our best interests in developing economies if we use our wealth to build, and grow, and to actually *make* something, and not to simply flush it all down the drain of superficial materialism. We are interested in helping business owners and other Glamour Globals become not just people who buy pretty suits and drive the right cars, blindly pursuing prestige, but who build brands and products that stand the test of time, taking their rightful place in the economy and reaping the rewards that naturally come with bringing value.

From a marketing perspective, Glamour Globals are loyal to trends rather than to brands. That is, they center their primary concern heavily on status and not on companies or products. They tend to follow only brands that already have a sizable following, and to drop those brands once opinion leaders have moved on. These consumers are unconscious spenders, with few concerns other than cultivating social status and indulging other narrowly selfish needs.

It is for this reason that we, myself and my co-authors, Miriam Mossalli, Yasmine Khashogji and Rola Ashour, hope to devote a good deal of our time and energy in this book into investigating ways that these Glamour Globals can come to a more mature way of thinking about consuming—about dealing with money, goods, and business. This, we will conclude, must be a process that starts with values.

We strongly believe that our lives, our economies, and our cultures will all be better served—and will be more prosperous for all—if strong, thoughtful values become a more vital part of our consumption discussions and decisions. We also believe that values are nurtured most profitably in the family.

The most important consideration in addressing the problem of new global wealth, as in everything else, is what we teach our children, and especially the behavior we model for them. In short, the best way to simmer down the Glamour Globals is to start thinking about how we might begin to live better lives as consumers, even given the blessed misfortune of having suddenly become immensely wealthy.

Thus, from my perspective and the unique vantage points of my co-authors, this book addresses the cultural, economic, and social problem of the "Glamour Globals"—people from developing countries who have suddenly come into wealth, and who are seemingly locked into a pattern of conspicuous consumption.

This audience poses a problem from a marketing perspective, because it tends to follow trends, rather than brands, and to make consumption decisions irrationally. We hope to suggest that opinion leaders in the developing world should begin to bring a discussion of values to the table as we think about consumption, in the hopes of ensuring a future that is both more prosperous and more fundamentally productive for all.

Chapter Two:
Who Are the Glamour Globals?

GLAMOUR GLOBALS ARE NOT OF any one race, ethnicity, religion, gender, or political inclination or organization. The term basically describes the behavior of people with a distinct worldview which emerged primarily as a result of the struggle between communism and capitalism.

Through the heart of the previous century, communistic regimes directly competed with capitalism regimes, with both forces, led by their respective superpowers, the United States and the Soviet Union, seeking countries in the third world and elsewhere which they could convince or compel to follow their respective political agendas. In this important way, it must be said, the two sides were similar. The world was torn between sectors and governmental bodies, with the result that a few countries opted to follow the communist regime and a few others decided to follow the capitalist.

Many Glamour Globals emerged from developing countries or emerging markets as a result of military rule. They were raised in an environment that instilled in them the belief that the power of money is the ultimate power, and that to buy into things is the most valid way to ensure the value of one's existence. The influence of the communist regime has had a very negative impact on the populations of these countries, placing them under one rule after the failure of democracy. That experience changed the behavior of the population from homespun modesty to an embrace of aggression at any cost.

A second group of Glamour Globals emerged under the influence of US capitalist interests, particularly in the Middle East, Africa and Pacific Asia, as people were newly plunged into modern life from their primitive days of not so long ago. Another important capitalistic spawning ground of Glamour Globals has been the US Diversified Visa (DV), granted to 55,000 people around the world from third world countries, under which people from developing nations around the world have been frequently exposed to and entranced by the material wealth of the West.

Emerging Markets: The Home of the Glamour Globals

The emerging markets are made up of those countries that have recently—that is, over the past three decades—witnessed rapid growth and industrialization. Many nations may be placed in this group, but four nations in particular, Brazil, Russia, India and China, collectively known as the BRIC states, are witnessing incredible growth. Aside from these nations, numerous others in Asia, Africa and the Middle East we may number among the twenty-eight nations designated in 2006 as emerging markets.

We will avoid the technical issue of illustrating further details of emerging markets and focus more on one noteworthy result that these emerging markets have produced: a very distinctive audience— the Glamour Globals. When we look at the emerging markets, we see both the advanced emerging markets represented by Brazil, Russia, India, and China, and the secondary emerging markets represented by such countries as Turkey, Egypt, South Africa and so on. These emerging markets have been a blessing to the world economy, as the governing bodies of many of those countries have worked furiously to advance their economies and create opportunities under which their citizens may flourish.

The development of some of these emerging market nations has continued, although a few have slowed recently due to the sting of such political turmoil as the protests in Egypt, Tunisia and elsewhere. Most recently, the *Economist* and the S&P have been studying the opportunity represented by such advancing nations and emerging markets as the United Arab Emirates, Qatar and Jordan. Development in these nations could offer more room for opportunity regionally in the Middle East as the number of emerging nations there would increase to rival that of Africa. Thus, certain questions arise: What will the future of these emerging markets look like? What will be the characteristics of the audience that comes from these markets?

CHAPTER THREE:

THE GLAMOUR GLOBALS AS A MARKETING PROBLEM

OVER THE PAST TWO DECADES, I have come to experience a new audience, found mostly in developing countries, in which a majority of the population is quite illiterate, but in which, meanwhile, many people among the upper class appear to be high on their wealth. This particular audience is very important for marketers to tap into, but they also present marketers with a range of unique dilemmas.

Of all the problems presented by this group, the most pressing, in my view, is that the Glamour Globals are loyal to hardly any brands, but are all about the latest trends. This audience is easy to please, but hard to control when it comes to creating a union between them and a brand. Another problem is that they can be quite irrational in their buying behavior.

Underlying this distinction is a very important trait of the Glamour Globals that we marketers must acknowledge and tackle for this audience: the apparently low self-esteem that most in this segment seem to suffer from. This low self-esteem is the underpinning of the group's tendency toward conspicuous consumption: making purchase decisions as a form of aggression, based on a desire to bolster their social status. This chronic problem is often characterized by impulsive purchase behavior, which may include the purchase of reputable fashion brands, but may also include latching onto anything that might temporarily inflate their egos by bolstering their social status. In the most vivid example of conspicuous consumption, among the Glamour Globals there appears to be a considerable amount of satisfaction derived merely from the amount they spend rather than the quality or utility of the goods they buy.

Perhaps it goes without saying that the problem of conspicuous consumption and ego buying is not restricted to the wealthy. Given the nature of conspicuous consumption as an outcome of low self-esteem, many people of average to slightly above average means have striven to join the Glamour Globals. These people have been too easily inspired by the above-average earners in their regions and they fully intend to follow their footsteps.

One of the most negative aspects of the Glamour Globals audience, given their tendency toward conspicuous consumption, is that they can quickly descend into negative thinking about almost everything; they can be very brutally aggressive to fellow human beings as they seek to earn their self-gratification. This audience, with the desire for status occupying so much of their attention, and their efforts to vie for status taking so much of their time, shows very little concern for education, culture, and many of the things which for calmer minds make life worth living.

Quite unfortunately, the Glamour Globals' obsession with status and hierarchy is not limited to material things. Their condition frequently results in their harboring bigotry against all human races, except for the superior race of their perception, namely their own. Money and material possessions are the cornerstones of their lives, and the only thing, they believe, that speaks to their true being and brings them value.

The Glamour Globals and Brands

With the unique characteristics of the Glamour Globals thus established, we can turn our attention to the peculiar way this audience encounters brands. In my work, I am a champion of the importance of brands, given that for most of the free-market world, brands are of paramount importance to both consumers and businesses. The marketing puzzle offered by this group, which seems to have such little regard for brands, is what first drew my attention to them as a subject of inquiry. In some ways, I view their disregard for brands as an outgrowth of their apparent disregard for other sources of value that most people hold dear, such as the importance of family, community, and the common good.

The Glamour Globals memorize brands, and they take every opportunity they can to flash them, on the t-shirts they wear, or on their social media profiles. But this attention to brand names is not a relationship with a brand in the way marketers have commonly come to conceive of consumer relationships with brands. It's almost as though these consumers were using brands by faking an association with them, in the same way that some unscrupulous people might forge a friendship for their own benefit.

The obsession of the Glamour Globals with the materialistic and superficial tends to overtake their interest in many things in which most of us might find deeper sources other than brands. Take for instance, the way I have observed that Glamour Globals travel.

When the Glamour Globals plan a weekend abroad, they make sure their hotels are close to the malls. Their preferred destinations are of course the most branded European and US cities: New York, Paris, London, Rome. Other places, no matter how rich with beauty and culture, if they lack an obvious ring of material prestige, may as well not exist for these jet-setters. They tend to visit the same cities a half-dozen times a year, and perhaps fifty times in ten years. The yellow brick road of materially wealthy major cities is the only world they know, and they apparently refuse to look beyond it.

Another quirk that Glamour Globals show with regard to travel is how they tend to memorize such things as the names of the hotels they stay in. In part, this is so because they look at hotels purely in terms of their names and brand names. They have no apparent experience with luxury ethics. Money is synonymous with luxury; money is not an avenue to culture or even the experience of living. They can pass the day in hours of intense shopping, and then go to restaurants, memorize the names of the items on the menu and post them on Twitter or Facebook.

For the Glamour Globals, the influence of conspicuous consumption extends beyond their purchase decisions, and their leisure choices, to encompass their very careers. Glamour Globals tend to base their careers and career aspirations on what looks to be the trendy occupation for the next few years. They may aspire to be a graphic designer for instance, or a brander, an art gallery artist, or a writer. Some may aspire to pursue more than one trendy profession at a time. It's not unusual for a Glamour Global to claim he or she is a fashion designer while unable to draw the simplest design or sew the most basic stitch. A few can claim to be anything you might imagine, as long as the job they are laying claim to fills their purpose of establishing their status within their society and community.

In my view it is easy—probably too easy—to lure this sort of target audience into committing excessive spending based on the fact that you could create or build a brand that would play upon their aspirations for an improved sense of self. One could easily offer a marketing ploy by which one invites Glamour Globals to belong in a circle that will elevate their status and their sense of satisfaction. I think, however, that we marketers would do well to consider that this type of audience lacks any sort of loyalty to brands, as to friendship. They have a single objective at any cost, and that is their social status, which they see as being identical to material acquisition.

Chapter Four:
Glamour Globals as a Demographic

ONCE WE ESTABLISH THE MARKETING problem posed by the Glamour Globals, it becomes a matter of some importance to draw some conclusions as to their characteristics as a demographic group. Although the Glamour Globals are a diverse group in some respects, they also share many important demographic characteristics.

When were Glamour Globals born?

This target audience, unique to the developing world, was typically born during the political and economical changes of the mid-50s. They were shaped economically in the early seventies, so that it has been almost forty years now since this audience's view of money and finances was shaped. The Glamour Globals thus had their origins during the cold war between the two superpowers, the US and the USSR, during which other countries around the world followed the lead of the two juggernauts in world political platforms.

The divisions wrought by this conflict of course remain to this day. The schisms among nations frequently began as the superpowers, especially the Soviet Union, helped create military regimes that adhered to the forms of the old tyrannical communist rule in many of the developing countries and in Africa. So deep were the grievances of many of the military rulers against the previous monarchies that they felt that cultivating hate was a viable way to help them build a new system, and they intentionally created and embedded certain forms of hatred and distrust in the minds of their populations. This sort of attitude has continued and spread throughout the years until, to this very day, people continue to inherit hateful attitudes and behaviors from their parents and pass them along to their children.

It is easy to view the story of the past forty to sixty years as being the tale of how the human essence of love and caring vanished, and the central role of materialism, hate and war burst on the stage. The Glamour Globals were born and nurtured under this school of thought. Meanwhile, the military leaders of previous regimes, as in much of the Middle East, Africa and Asia, clung to power regardless of the cost in terms of human loss.

Thus, the demographic origins of the Glamour Globals set into motion both their deep anxieties and their profound regard for whatever might best enhance their perceived social status, causing them to virtually ignore any sense of obligation to be of service to humanity

The Glamour Globals are the world's fast growing population in terms of both their buying behavior and the amount they spend.

Where are Glamour Globals found?

Glamour Globals are not a phenomenon of any country in particular, or indeed of any handful of countries. They can be found all over the world, including much of the Middle East, Africa, China, South Asia, Europe and the US. The US and Europe in the past forty years have witnessed the growth of this population, springing from former communist regimes after the collapse of those regimes in the early and mid-nineties. A huge number of Glamour Globals control much of the growing wealth in South Asia and China, while another sizable population can be found in Middle East and Africa.

In terms of the countries from which Glamour Globals come, China represents an excellent example and potential case study. Over the past two to three decades, China has ridden a sudden economic ascent that fertilized the lives of the Chinese people after the rigid rule of the past. China's liberalizing of economic policies has helped many Chinese people enjoy a life different from what they had been used to, so the Chinese people have been eager to enter the world of brands and trends. The Chinese people experiencing wealth for the first time have been glamorized by the lure of the West, away from their core traditions and toward a life of a new kind of social acceptance. Another good example is the case of the Middle East and Africa, where English has emerged as a widely spoken language of commerce, to the extent that one can well imagine that in a few decades the number of English speakers may surpass the number of Arabic and local African dialects. The sort of social class distinction that most seek is one that their parents and grandparents never lived, one profoundly marked by the Western influence. A low self-opinion has led many Middle Easterners to follow trends while still maintaining parts of their local culture and a few traditions dressed in Western perceptions. This situation has placed this audience well within the phenomenon of the Glamour Globals.

In general, most Glamour Globals live in areas which have recently witnessed rapid economic growth. A few have also fallen from the tree of communism and migrated to such Western regions as the US and Europe.

WHAT ARE SOME SALIENT DEMOGRAPHIC FEATURES OF THE GLAMOUR GLOBALS?

The type of audience behavior that we have been discussing in this book usually starts around the age of sixteen. Most Glamour Globals have been profoundly influenced by their parents' school of thought and by the nature of the countries they live in. The majority of Glamour Globals now are between the ages of sixteen and fifty. A few revert to their true nature once they've reached the wisdom of knowing who they are. They tend to be homeowners and seek the sort of lifestyles that they and even their parents were once denied. The emotional demands of being in or qualifying for a certain social class drives this target audience to spend beyond the norm. Their key goal is social acceptance, and they think of little else. They have only superficial loyalty to friends and family. They tend to gear their thoughts toward things that will bring purely personal benefit or give them the social clout to which they aspire. Glamour Globals are behavior- and action-driven people who tend to change constantly, because in the past they've lacked all the elements they desired which they thought could push them forward.

How fast are Glamour Globals growing?

I don't have the statistics to determine the size of this population, nor did I conduct the research necessary to find out, but one thing we may say for sure based on common sense: Any area on this planet which sees a substantial change in its political and economical climate will certainly invite a renewed presence of Glamour Globals. Given that China is now one of the leading countries in the world, and given China's huge population growth rate, the emergence of Glamour Globals there has been exceptional. That growth has not been based on the size of the Chinese population, but on the ever-increasing adoption of the Glamour-Global lifestyle.

When we see such behavior as a skyscraper being built in the middle of nowhere, employing thousands of people, but paying them less than a dollar a day, while forcing them to live in conditions of squalor, we are observing the behavior of Glamour Globals who seek to serve themselves and not humanity. Such behavior is everywhere in evidence, and it shows every sign of being easy to hand down from generation to generation. The growth of the population of Glamour Globals is unavoidable; Glamour Global behavior is spreading fast from place to place around the world. Each year, it seems, the occurrence of this sort of behavior doubles, until the world begins to look quite strange compared to the world that many of us knew, or thought we knew, only a few decades ago.

Chapter Five:
Glamour Globalism

Glamour Globalism, if we may coin that phrase, is a sort of behavior that we have seen emerging in the developing world over the past sixty years in the course of some of those countries joining the ranks of the emerging markets. As mentioned above, the political broil that was the result of the conflict between the two superpowers in the cold war era, between the capitalist and communist philosophies, and amid the competitive efforts of the superpowers to win various countries to either side of the great divide, was the breeding ground of the behavior of the Glamour Globals.

Many examples of the Glamour Globalism spring to mind, but prominent among these is the change of the political platforms in countries such as Egypt, from monarchy to military dictatorships supported by the previous Soviet regime. That sort of situation gave birth to new behavioral impulses which arose from a desire to retaliate against the wealthy society of the era of the Egyptian monarchy. Efforts to indulge that impulse toward retaliation were led by a few soldiers who took power as rulers and leaders of the country. These leaders passed their hatred on to the general public, who were, however, deprived of the opportunity to practice similar behaviors and indulge similar impulses of their own in public. Years passed and those who had lived under the monarchy moved to countries in the West to flourish, leaving all the best that had been built evincing a more noble essence to be demolished under the influence of hate.

Under this abiding ethos of disdain and hate for what has gone before, today one may find many among the new rich who, for generation after generation, have clung to only one school of thought: the conviction that one should hate everything the previous generation has produced. Given their lack of ethical fundamentals, the Glamour Globals of Egypt have sought only to adopt the lifestyle of the previous society under the Egyptian monarchy, one which never fit the country well in the first place due to its own absence of the fundamentals necessary to polish a lifestyle and make it a good fit.

Such behavior has only given rise to abuses of wealth and an ever more zealous quest for social acceptance. For example, speaking English in the Arab world qualifies a person to be from the upper society. Being able to portray someone from that layer of the culture does not always open the gates to the desired areas.

The chronic lack of self-acceptance among the Glamour Globals has created a pressure on their souls to be aggressive at all costs to reach the pinnacle of society, to strike the proper pose. From my perspective, while many might take references to having a heritage of tents and camels as an insult, to me such an acknowledgment is no insult. It is simply the reality of the prevailing lifestyle of this certain geographical area until recent years. I'm descended from a tribe named Baaghil that migrated from Hadramouth in the Arabian peninsula to other parts of the world. I'm very fond of my heritage and display it proudly amongst my friends and in public.

Now to transform one's habits and nature from rural roots to modern urban lifestyles should be a matter for gradual growth as people learn to grapple with new realities. Today the society of these countries finds itself in a state of confusion, caught between tradition and perception, with perception generally emerging as the rule of thumb as people make decisions.

These trends imply that most of these countries have a sizable population which indulges itself in Glamour Globalism. In the case of China the sudden growth that China has witnessed over the past three decades has only made room for the birth of the Glamour Globals. Behavior has transformed from modest to aggressive at any cost. The core objective of the Glamour Globals of China is to be socially accepted globally and locally. They have become very materialistic and brand oriented, to the point that LV and other world fashion brands have had to set a queue rule outside their doors on Canton road in Hong Kong, and to the point that if you speak to just a few of them, you quickly learn that their leisure activity is shopping and only shopping.

Having thus painted the behavior of the Glamour Globals in broad strokes, it may be useful to list a few interesting particulars of their behavior in various areas.

Idol language. English has become the language to speak—the one which one must learn in order to be socially accepted. It serves the high side of society such that most look on the acquisition of English as a rising trend.

Children. The Glamour Globals make sure that their children are very presentable, dressing them in Western attire, and letting the nanny teach them English, since the mother generally can't speak a word of it.

Leisure time. Their preferred areas tend to be prime shopping districts and restaurants, where they meet with friends and gossip about other friends. While they are not brand loyal, they certainly do shop, following the latest trends, specifically those that designers unveil in New York, London and Paris each year. By contrast, there will occasionally be someone who is highly loyal to Ralph Lauren, the Gap, or the like, and who will consistently buy from those designers even if they're out of fashion. Glamour Globals care more about what's out today than the brand's essence.

Opinion leaders. Glamour Globals will easily follow a community leader who sets trends, perhaps a popular person who produces videos or someone known to be a social media addict.

Trending. The Glamour Globals relate more to the world of fashion than to style, even though style lives and fashion dies. They'll follow any sort of trend that is transformed into a product or that a select few pick up and a few others follow. They themselves will only follow a trend if the numbers of followers are on the increase. To them, quality or other sources of value do not figure in to how they value the trend. Its very trendiness is their primary concern.

Learning. Glamour Globals offer pretences as to the importance of knowledge, but they seldom trouble themselves to live it. The word *educated* has become a trend word which they employ freely, although it is an opportunity they rarely benefit from in any real sense.

Brands vs. trends. Glamour Globals are highly loyal to trends. They are able to name brands, but they are more acquainted with the trend, in terms of what's in and out. In the world of fashion, Glamour Globals may look at those brands that consistently produce trends: Armani, Louis Vuitton, or any of a host of European brands. To move the discussion from fashion to consumer goods, Glamour Globals are likely to use iPhones because they are the in thing to own, until Samsung becomes the in thing. This sort of brand-hopping to follow trends is how things work in most emerging markets.

Buying. Glamour Globals spend primarily to show how wealthy they are. In many cases in the Middle East, most of their spending is simply wasted, while it might be said that more people in China, the BRIC states and Africa spend in pursuit of self-fulfillment.

Brands. Glamour Globals relate to brands only if they are fully endorsed by community leaders, friends and family.

Business decisions. Family opinion and the views of friends and wives account for a big chunk of the decision making of Glamour Globals. Their companies, when they own companies, are operated from home, and wives, who may be clueless concerning the business itself, can sometimes make dangerous decisions and influence her husband to take action on them.

Teamwork and loyalty. As employees, Glamour Globals tend to do only what their higher-ups say. Loyalty to the company among employees of small businesses and midsize companies is very rare. They tend to focus on how to win managers and others to their side, even when the other side is the company. Their title at work sometimes means more than their salary. Glamour Globals as business owners frequently take over someone's business to pay him off and not so that they can grow a business. They are focused more on how to earn today than how to build a company. Meanwhile, few Glamour Globals are visionaries. Areas like the BRIC states have spawned visionaries from among the generation of Glamour Globals, but not the Middle East.

PART II:

MIRIAM MOSALLI

CHAPTER SIX:
FASHION VS. TRENDS

"Fashions Fade, Style is Eternal"—Yves Saint Laurent

THE ABOVE QUOTE FROM FRENCH designer Yves Saint Laurent summarizes the difference between a fashion trend and an individual's style. The latter is innate within a person; in fact, it acts as an extension of that person's personality. It is his or her inner individuality expressed externally. Regardless of trends, the individual's style is constant and represents a growing consciousness of his or her likes and dislikes. The individual is more likely to remain loyal to such preferences, given that this kind of intentional selection makes people more secure and confident.

On the other end of the personality spectrum we find the Glamour Globals, a group Said has already explored in depth. As a fashion consultant, I am interested in how insecurity dominates this persona and is externally expressed through a need to fit in. This insecurity explains the Glamour Globals' impulse to follow fashion trends, instead of cultivating a consistent fashion style. Such individuals are trend followers, not trendsetters. They are highly dependent on the media to tell them what is "in." They follow blogs, read international fashion magazines, and look to celebrities to be their fashion icons. Their purchase decisions are made for them, not by them.

As Said has observed, Glamour Globals are not loyal to a certain brand; instead, they follow trends. In the fashion context, this means that they may not particularly like Céline, but will purchase the brand if the present trend stipulates that the "IT" bag of the season is in fact made by the French House. They like neon and spikes because the international fashion world tells them such is what they should like. Their preferences are incredibly malleable and can be easily manipulated through the media and celebrity endorsements. Quality and technical features of a product are void *ab initio,* as the Glamour Global's concerns begin and end with possessing a product that external sources have dictated is now in demand.

A Glamour Global, therefore, thinks *style* means always being *in* style, rather than possessing a signature fashion sense. The individual's style is seen to be one that is in sync with current trends. Unfortunately, the need to be *in* the trend does not push people to be *ahead* of the trends. They do not possess the confidence and fashion acumen to be fashion-forward or to set new trends. They follow trends blindly and base their decisions on a collective desire rather than on a personal preference.

CHAPTER SEVEN:
GLAMOUR GLOBALS AND BRAND SHOPPING

"Whoever said that money can't buy happiness, simply didn't know where to go shopping."— Bo Derek

THE CONSUMER BEHAVIOR OF A glamorized individual is unique. Glamour Globals are not like the mass-market audience, which also follows trends. Instead, they possess a more selective predisposition when it comes to trend following. The glamorized individual often wants what is hard to attain. In fact, the most important two words for such an individual are "Limited Edition." Ironically, they see themselves as part of an exclusive class and therefore, tend to lean toward exclusive items.

A few years ago BottegaVeneta created a special, limited edition version of the Stretch Knot handbag to celebrate the opening of the flagship store in Dubai. Available in a numbered edition of just 25, it was sold exclusively at the Mall of the Emirates Fashion Dome boutique. Made of lizard in a lush shade of fuchsia and embellished with corners sheathed in hand-woven intrecciato antique sterling silver, the "Dubai Knot" is an elegant variation on BottegaVeneta's celebrated Knot clutch, only with a slightly elongated shape that lends the bag a sleek and feminine silhouette. The description of its features becomes secondary to the main appeal: that it is a numbered limited edition for a specific region. Again, the Glamour Globals feel that possessing such an exclusive item makes them part of a premier, well traveled demographic.

As a luxury consultant, I often advise my clients to have the products they'd like to push hidden from public view. The Glamour Globals should be made to believe that the item is reserved for only an elite few and that they are special enough to be included. Another tactic is to have items appear to be flown in. Glamorized individuals tend to prefer to shop outside their local markets, as adding a flight further signifies their elitism. They want to be able to state that they purchased their items at one of the major fashion capitals than to reveal the items' accessibility to the public. Therefore, it is often smart for luxury brands to tell their clients that the item is unavailable, but can be shipped in order to be made exclusively available to them. "Upon Special Request" has become a magic phrase because if the product is not readily available, the item suddenly becomes more coveted. It's the golden rule of "We want what we can't have," or in this case, what we can't have immediately.

The glamorized audience is not about deals and discounts, but rather added value. Discounts appear demeaning to them because the price tag plays a significant role in the illusion of being part of an elite class. And the most important consideration for such an individual is to be seen by outsiders as being part of the top tier of the socio-economic hierarchy. For them, the bragging rights are almost as important—if not more important—than the actual purchase itself. This is where customization also comes in. Customization becomes a segue into the realm of the limited edition, which as mentioned earlier, is one of the key tenants of product desirability.

CHAPTER EIGHT:
HOW THE GLAMOUR GLOBAL DEFINES FASHION

"Fashion is made to become unfashionable." –Coco Chanel

THE DEFINITION OF FASHION TO the glamorized audience is fleeting. It is whatever is in trend, regardless of brand or added value. Whether we're talking about a car, a watch or a handbag, one thing is for sure: if it's expensive and visually marked with either a logo or signature product shapes, then it is desired.

Now, all that may sound a little superficial—and it is—but it's a well-accepted absolute truth among the Glamour Globals. In the present world, which is saturated in international designer goods, it's all about showing off to others the ability to buy what is expensive and new.

Emilio Pucci was one of the first designers to sell luxury as a lifestyle rather than a product. The Italian designer included this elite lifestyle in all his branding, giving his clientele an opportunity to buy a dream, rather than merely a simple, printed kaftan. For glamorized individuals, fashion represents a piece of this lifestyle, even though the lifestyle they are aspiring to attain is not connected to a particular brand or set of brands. Again, it is all about flaunting one's ability to buy whatever is currently trendy. In that way, the Glamour Globals demonstrate a classless sense of false luxury.

This phenomenon also explains the magic of the capsule collection.

Sofia Coppola for Louis Vuitton or their collaboration with the Japanese artist Takashi Murakami are all sought-after pieces, not because they bring more technical expertise or higher quality to the closet, but rather because their offerings are limited and the window of opportunity to purchase them creates a sense of immediacy. The glamorized individual wants these things because not everyone can have them. Fashion for them is wearing a false sense of entitlement that is literally what money can buy, rather than what taste or culture has bestowed upon you.

GLAMOUR GLOBAL CHARACTERISTICS: THE FASHION PERSPECTIVE

In what follows, I will approach a few of the idiosyncrasies of the Glamour Globals that Said mentioned, this time from my perspective as a luxury consultant, because we have observed that those same characteristics can manifest themselves quite differently and interestingly in the context of my area of expertise. Thus, I here view certain characteristics of the Glamour Globals as if they were fashion problems.

Pastimes. The favorite pastime of the Glamour Globals is any activity that they perceive to be aligned with the leisure class. Whether it's spending their time at a beach off the Côte d'Azur, skiing in Gstaad, riding horses, or shopping at high-end boutiques and flagship stores, these individuals believe that all their activities should reflect those of an elite class of privilege. Their activities by no means indicate a certain preference for such activities, but rather follow what is the latest fad. Much like their lack of brand loyalty, Glamour Globals will shift their favorite pastime activity to whichever activity is the most popular among the affluent demographic.

The Glamour Globals do engage in many social activities, as status among peers is their primary goal. Whether they are posting pictures on Facebook of their summer in Cannes, or showing off their latest fashion buys from Milan at a social gathering, the goal is to make sure their surrounding social sphere is well aware of their privileged exploits.

Learning. Glamour Globals perceive knowledge as a basis of self-advancement. Such individuals operate within a bubble of self-interest. Their knowledge is therefore limited to issues that directly affect the individual. Focusing on the immediate, such individuals fail to recognize precursors to subsequent affects. Worldly issues are taken into consideration only as they directly affect their current situation. Glamour Globals are oblivious of the financial anomalies that have made them the main focus of many brands. Instead, they believe that their position of wealth equates to a position of a bought "aristocracy" over everyone else.

Treatment of the Help. Glamour Globals see their domestic help as an extension of their affluent lifestyles. The domestic worker becomes an accessory of their elite status. The domestic workers are often considered and treated as being below human status, becoming almost extensions of the limbs of the individual to further elevate the employer's agenda.

Fears. Glamour Globals are highly insecure. Their need to fit in is the basis of most of their choices, whether it's buying a designer handbag, or traveling to a certain vacation destination. They will not buy knockoffs due to their limited acumen with the brand. They are unsure of the authentic characteristics of the brand, and this uncertainty increases their fear of being exposed by others as possessing an imitation.

Part III:

Yasmine Khashogji

CHAPTER NINE:
UNDERSTANDING THE DEVOTION TO TRENDS

OVER THE PAST THREE DECADES, a particular audience has emerged in developing markets. They are not loyal to brands; they are merely trend followers. This category of people is growing fast—they can be spotted almost everywhere. They have been known to be quite cognizant of their surroundings, and this awareness drives them to pull out all the stops to be popular. Their obsession with trend-following behavior is the predominant feature amongst them. Their dynamism is quite intense. And their ecstasy and comfort level with trend-setting is such that it prompts them to practice various schemes to socially "fit in." To sum it up, they are an audience loyal to trends over brands: The Glamour Globals.

Following Said's discussion of the identity of that group, and Marriam's discussion of their approach to the specific industry of fashion, my section of the book concerns itself with certain important aspects of their practices, starting with their devotion to trends, their globe trotting norms and activities, and a few solitary debates to support the keynote of Glamour Globals' behavior.

Let us start with the basics: Glamour Globals are trendoids—specifically to trends that have been generated by the crème de la crème. Aristocrats or plebeians alike have found themselves imprisoned in this collective tenor. Such behavior is not allied with a particular social status nor a financial accumulation. In order to feel better about themselves, they think that by riding the latest wave they will be more involved in this alluring clique and will be au courant—up-to-the-minute.

Two very important questions are worth raising here to clarify the Glamour Globals' devotion to trends. What is a trend? And what is a trend in the case of the Glamour Globals?

A trend is a mainstream orientation in which something is spreading or alternating. The behavior of trend-following could be defined as a phase that takes place across diverse demographics during three different time frames: long, medium, and short. Also, trends are variable in terms of who, what, where and when. In contemporary communities, how we observe trends has changed over time. People can now easily spot and observe trends no matter where they because of the abilities granted to them by the technological revolution. Today the new media have become the major resource that delivers trend messages—via blogs, social networks, TV, magazines, and simply smart phones applications. Trend-following has recently become a fundamental social necessity. Commonly in the past, trends were associated primarily with the fashion and beauty industry, but not anymore.

In the case of the Glamour Globals, trends are implemented according to the public mood of the elites. A classic case of shallowness! It is important to note, moreover, that trends, in the Glamour Global code of honor, are inevitably related exclusively to a way of life. Trends modify one's lifestyle as whole. Importantly, while Glamour Globals are profoundly influenced by trend following, many of them seem to be unaware that they are actually doing so. And in a different aspect of the story, Glamour Globals strive for affiliation with trend pioneers. Their devotion to trends is taken to a different stage and their self-assurance would potentially be under threat if they were not a part of the live, hip trend.

Many would question why it is consequential to comply with such an ideology—simply to be a person who's interested in the scoop? As I mentioned in my introduction and as the book's tagline suggests, Glamour Globals are an audience loyal to trends over brands. That quality alone ultimately classifies an individual into this coterie. Such behavioral adherence places a great number of brands in danger of fluctuating and falling flat.

Glamour Globals' trends are miscellaneous. They can involve education, fashion, travel, health, psychology and many other worldly components. Trends originate and re-form from basic sources, but Glamour Globals have their mystical ways of utilizing and exposing trends.

One of the most conspicuous trends among Glamour Globals is associated with the educational sphere. As an illustration, a certain part of the populace sends its children to bourgeois educational institutes because of an inability to afford ritzy ones. The children mix and mingle with a society they have been exposed to all their lives. In the final stage of their educational experience, parents relocate them to that ritzy school to make them a part of elite society. This move naturally creates massive chaos in a child's life, engendering intellectual mismatch. These parents take such a biased measure to prepare the children to enter the world of Glamour Globals—the synthetic world.

Chapter Ten:
Glamour Globe Trotting

ONE AREA IN WHICH TREND-FOLLOWING emerges seemingly on a subconscious level is in the area of travel choices. Glamour Globals are obsessed with travel. Globe-trotting is their flavor of the month. To elucidate their travel protocol, I will embark on their quintessential travel action plan. Customarily, they prefer the most desired locations, attractions and times of year, of course when prices are highest. Naturally, hardcore shopping comes on the heels of the plan in alignment with the happening. Standing in front of closets and piled purchases, they head-scratch over the choice of what to pack and what not to. The aftermath of this and that is dozens of suitcases stacked in terminals, not to mention last-minute arrivals and check-ins. During the departure process, not a moment is wasted— Glamour Global flair at its finest!

Among the many factors encouraging Glamour Globals to travel, shopping remains one of the most significant. The world of fashion attracts them, and they go far beyond the mind's eye to adhere to its trends. One very visible way this trend-following emerges is on social media, through shared images of daily outfits, in which the wearer names the brand of each piece he or she is wearing. Through their fashionista displays, they inspire other Glamour Globals who are obsessed with world of fashion.

Apparently, attendance at fashion weeks is a must among the Glamour Globals, although these travelers are not part of the fashion industry. Fashion has become an aspiration for them. In their mindset, involvement is merely a matter of presence, nothing more and nothing less. When appearing at such events, they once again try their best to get their presence noticed through social media—Foursquare for checking in, Facebook for posts and updates, and recently, the trend of Instagram for sharing snapshots. Another reason behind such visits is so Glamour Globals can possess the sort of "Limited/Special edition" productions Marriam mentioned previously. This trend is in keeping with the unique qualities of the process of forethought of the Glamour Globals.

Fashion capitals or branded cities grab many other travelers not only for the fashion, but for the inviting weather, the historical architecture, and the exquisite local food. The case of the Glamour Globals, however, is different. They are always found in the hot spots, or as I would refer to them, "the gravitational locales." They are endlessly attracted to whereabouts that have been recommended by other Glamour Globals.

How can we spot a Glamour Global?

Each and every city around the world has its "hangout" list. Grammar Globals can be found in most high-end boulevards where upscale boutiques are located, wearing voguish attires. They tend to visit specific restaurants and order specific dishes as suggested, taking snapshots of their food which they then post on social media to acknowledge the recommendations they've received—especially when it comes to dessert! As a result, a portion of those genuine industries have been converted into volume industries and have lost their authenticity in an unfortunate result of the star-struck wannabe behavior of Glamour Globals.

Moreover, each country has a unique culture with its own customs and traditions. Among many Japanese tourists, for example, photography is a major aspect of travel. This trend has expanded throughout many countries, especially the Middle East. It is quite typical to find Glamour Globals carrying professional DSLR cameras with them everywhere, even though those cameras are weighty and irritating to carry at times. It is still worth the hassle! The users of such cameras have no prior coaching nor expertise, and the camera is generally on "auto" mode, yet the right camera is simply indispensable! You may find them capturing still images of clouds, flowers, paintings, monuments, or just random shots of street signs.

Another trend that has transferred from another culture is the football craze. Glamour Globals travel to attend football games and to visit football arenas. They are quite likely only "glory supporters." They will follow a famous player from team to team with no acknowledgement of the teams, their history or their achievements. They'll travel miles and spend a fortune on tickets just to be seen at a game. Moreover, they share their check-ins, photos, and live tweets on social media. Such participation contradicts the true essence of loyal football fans who have been supporters almost all their lives, if not having inherited their fan allegiance from previous generations.

A major drift of the Glamour Globals' travel drill is the language digest. They learn by rote various colloquialisms of the many countries they have visited to practice on their compeers. Using simple words such as "Ciao," "Bonjour," "Hola," and so on allows them to tout their bilingualism and to feel multicultural. This perception is definitely another breakout of the Glamour Globals' discipline of belonging.

Among the various travel rituals of Glamour Globals, the constant hunt for business franchises is another common scenario. For each new place they visit, they discuss its potential business opportunities and bountiful outcomes. Unaware of market demand or surpluses, they remain confident of their decisions. The primary motive behind such deliberations is fame, but of course who would mind affluence?

When it is almost time for the Glamour Globals to return home, they bear a load of mementos for their loved ones. These are not Eiffel tower figurines, or I LOVE NEW YORK t-shirts, or an Empire State Building glass ball, or even those Russian matryoksha dolls. Forget the clichéd travel souvenirs! Souvenirs are now very turgid. They vary from Ladurée macaroons, Bobby Brown makeup kits, Godiva chocolate boxes up to Tom Ford eau de colognes. Moreover, why go for bargains when cash is superfluous? Such gifts are still further evidence of the Glamour Globals' mindset, the constant striving for attention and the lax logic.

To finish off the vacation, Glamour Globals have a checklist of the "must" visit places. And these are literally musts for them, even if the list has no intrinsic interest to them. This programmed travel routine is surprisingly unsurprising. Such other-driven decision-making is a significant reflection of the inner psychology at work, and of the lengths these people will go to in order to fit in with the nouveau riche circle.

Although we can now predict their characteristics as travelers, we still cannot be certain what will be next for them. Generally speaking, their ongoing change serves them well based on this inner vacancy of self esteem. This stereotypical behavior does not reflect a certain culture; it *is* the culture of Glamour Globals. Their customs are quite structured, not to mention rather trivial. Glamour Globals are disciplined in following the trends they identify. Their travel borders expand, with countries around the Middle East and Far East becoming new vacation hot spots. Thus, following the trends, they will be always on the go, depending on their state of mind.

CHAPTER ELEVEN:
GLAMOUR GLOBALS UNLEASHED

AMONG THE GLOBE TROTTERS I surveyed, many chose summer over winter as their preferred travel time because it is the priciest season of the year, thus allowing them to practice the attitude Said described perfectly in Chapter Five. This preference reflects the mindset of many communities, especially the youth. They seem to want to travel constantly, whether they need to or not. Their eternal feeling of boredom explains this unjustifiable perspective.

In several ways, travel trends seemed to vary between men and women. A popular view among the men surveyed was that that they preferred traveling on short breaks, with friends, sharing rooms in luxury hotels. The hotel should be located in the heart of the city. A luxury car must accompany this package for the negligible transport. They typically prefer visiting loud cities with beaches, such as Marbella, Miami, Mykonos, Ibiza, Cannes and Bodrum, during peak holiday times. They also plan vacations after obsessive Internet research, looking for the best parties of that year. Shopping, on the other hand, is always a part of the vacation. A noticeable trend before travel is posting questions on Facebook and Twitter to acquire as much information as possible about the city they will be visiting.

By contrast, most of the women surveyed said they most enjoy shopping when they travel. They tend to ask each other about the best local boutiques, preferring them to well-known brands. Their favored cities are Paris, London, Milan, New York, Barcelona, Istanbul and

Beirut. They prefer long vacations of more than a month, mostly during winter and fall. Many prefer to travel with their families (parents/ siblings/husbands), and just a few enjoy traveling with their friends or alone. Other women, such as mothers and workers, prefer relaxing breaks which allow them to escape their responsibilities. Most choose less crowded cities such as the Maldives, Bali, Bombay, Prague, and various islands in Thailand, where they stay in super luxurious spas to be indulged and pampered. The women I interviewed reported sleeping up to 10 hours per night on vacation.

Families expressed a range of opinions. More than one family consisting of a married couple and a newborn preferred calmer vacations, mostly choosing such places as Geneva, Boston, and Florence. They see the perfect vacation destination as a place that has it all: good food, parks and shopping. Other families consisting of members of various ages favored traveling to cities convenient to all of them, such as London, Kuala Lumpur, Barcelona and various states in America. They usually travel during summer, spending six weeks doing so, on average. Their travel activities are mostly shopping, eating and sightseeing. The perfect duration of their travel is two to three weeks.

The spectrum of opinion I encountered through my survey demonstrated a staggering result: From their point of view, traveling serves as a getaway from the flavorless routine of their daily lives in addition to giving them another means of achieving status and the recognition of their peers.

Unfortunately, the Glamour Globals tend to be very prejudiced about their standards. They quite regard themselves as the cream of the cream, and they look at outsiders as the unsophisticated public. Wealth, fame, and the finer things of the world remain their foremost concern in a way that one might well find to be a perfect example of abhorrent materialism.

PART IV:

ROLA ASHOUR

CHAPTER TWELVE:
HOW DID THE STORY START AND WHY?

THIS IS WHERE I, ROLA Ashour, a lecturer of psychology, will tackle the issue at hand: The issue of the *Glamour Globals*, conspicuous consumers, nouveau riche, parvenu...all different names given to the same group of people.

I am alarmed in particular at the crisis in self-esteem that has emerged; a crisis which clearly underlies the problem of conspicuous consumption that besets this population. Thus, in this section of the book, I will explore the prospects for the Glamour Globals to develop as consumers, and I will offer, I hope, some paths forward in that regard. To that end, I will focus initially on the role of the family as a conduit for building healthy self-esteem, and second, I will emphasize teaching children better values related to consumption, as well as the role of school and environment.

I will start by mentioning a British television series, "Downton Abbey," that I have recently watched and that reflects exactly how old are the reasons behind the twin problems of status and segregation. Throughout history people have been divided into classes. Segregation has been clear-cut, and movement between the classes has been difficult if not impossible to achieve. For those who have not watched the show, it talks about the story of a well-to-do old English family and their servants: upstairs and downstairs.

I will use only one example from Downtown Abbey to explain how hard, if not impossible, it is to reach the status of acceptance. I am not justifying the lifestyles of these people, but attempting to help you understand the why and/or how Glamour Globals may have arisen. The show tells the story of two men during World War I, dependent on each other, but more importantly equal to each other—brothers in arms, as they say. Yet life can be very harsh. When the war ends, each returns to his birthright regardless of his efforts and irrelevant to the wealth each has accumulated. One is the master, and the other, a mere servant.

Now let's take this idea and look at its mirror image in today's world.

To stay with the British theme, it was obvious in the 90's that no matter how much wealth one may have amassed, the *"old money"* would never open its doors to you, let alone let you in.

Deflated, angry and devoid of any meaningful ambition, the nouveau riche turned towards another group of people: the stars and the actors. Their motivation has now become to imitate the dress code, style and way of life of their famous counterparts.

Gone were the values of true self worth, hard work, humbleness and real manners in favor of flashiness, extravagance and loud behavior. These, among others, have become the new characteristics most often encountered in the parvenus.

The question that now arises is what was the order of evolution that led to the Glamour Globals' final need for a defined status? Or their need to survive and achieve fulfillment?

I will not discuss how capitalism or communism has left many countries in deprivation and how it led to the rise of the Glamour Globals, nor will I discuss the new world order and the emerging markets, but I will discuss the internal purpose or psychological reasons behind their emergence.

Let's start with status. What is status and why do we give it so much importance? Those are questions that a great many researchers, psychologists and psychometricians, just to name a few, have been eager to find answers for.

STATUS

In general, *status* is the term used to define one's relation to wealth and the power granted by that wealth. The need for status explains why throughout the generations we have seen the upper class claiming knowledge, moral superiority and honor. The "savoir vivre" is their birthright based on proper breeding. Social integration between the classes based on wealth has been difficult, prolonging and strengthening the stereotype, rendering it a vicious circle; the people who belonged to the *nouveau riche* wanted to belong but were not accepted by the upper classes, so they turned to loudness and conspicuous consumption believing that such behavior would give them a place in those elite circles. They began imitating *old money* by donating to certain causes. Giving alms is something people from "proper breeding" have always done, but when the nouveau riche put their feet on such a route, people from *old money* describe it as flaunting their wealth or condescending toward the needy.

Nevertheless, these behaviors have led to the belief that money permits one to obtain not only status and possessions, but also power and control over others. In replication, this belief contributes to increased materialism and expressions of vanity amongst the Glamour Globals. These behaviors may resonate well with consumers, but we cannot believe that pleasure and happiness are the sole values that govern our wellbeing in life. If we do so, then we will justify materialism and vanity, creating an ethical problem and encouraging compulsive buying. Why is all of this so? Again, it's a vicious circle that the Glamour Globals find themselves in. The more they buy, the more possessions will give them a sense of status or power, the vainer they become, and thus the circle is completed as these consumers compulsively buy. The Glamour Globals develop their characteristics and their attitudes towards money because of the sense of importance they experience in its presence.

ATTITUDE TOWARDS MONEY

Attitudes consist of the way we think about something and how we behave based on those perceptions. We have attitudes towards fashion, religion, education, and so on. One concept I will discuss here is attitudes toward money. Some believe money is central to their existence; others believe it is meant to increase possessions and provide us with more materialistic possessions. Our attitudes are learned behaviors that we have amassed while growing up in our environment. We imitate our parents and how they relate to money, and we are also influenced by those in our immediate surroundings. Those experiences are the main factors that will influence our attitudes towards money as adults. For example, many people who grew up during the cold war have learned the hard way the importance of savings; thus, today they tend to be less thrifty than individuals born in different environments.

We need to acquire a better understanding of our perceptions of our finances. A negative attitude towards money can cause individuals and society at large to behave erratically or to become more depressed and less satisfied with life and with what it has offered them. Such responses occur when people's self-worth is tied to their net worth.

What is great about our attitude toward money is that because it is a learned behavior, it can be changed with proper dedication, hard work and motivation. Money is basically defined from birth by our parents, the society we live in and the friends we make, among other influences. How those entities view money determines whether we see it as a means to get what we want in terms of the necessities of life or whether we see it as a way to show others where we stand in terms of status and to give us self esteem. Once we have built our attitude towards the financial aspect of our lives we will tend to display behaviors accordingly. When we are dissatisfied with ourselves and our image we can work hard to change that image. However, we need to be consciously aware that we truly need such change in order to become fulfilled on a deeper level.

We also need to understand why we strive for status, why we want to attain status and why we believe we will find happiness and fulfillment through the attainment of high status. Human beings have to be motivated in order to spend time and persevere in anything they do. Let's have a look at what motivation is and how it influences our entire being.

MOTIVATION

In 1943, Abraham Maslow authored his theory of motivation, in which he identified the primary forces behind our motivation in terms of five levels of basic needs. Those needs are essential; they are the driving force behind our achievement. Once we have reached the pinnacle of the pyramid we can achieve our fullest potential. Humanity by nature strives to achieve. Maslow created a pyramid to classify these needs in order of importance: Survival, Safety, Social, Esteem and Fulfillment. At the lowest level of the pyramid, people are motivated to fulfill their basic biological needs, such as shelter and food. Having secured our survival, we need to fulfill our need for safety, and then our need for love and esteem. Once the lower-level needs have been met, we move on to the need of fulfilling our individual potential. Our primary motivator becomes an innate need for self-actualization. On a basic level, we need to become everything we are capable of becoming.

When we view status from Maslow's perspective, we realize that it is an esteem need, and regardless of where we fall on the economic ladder, we all generally strive to achieve status before we can move on to the highest need. We are social creatures. As to the question of whether nature or nurture is primarily responsible for our drives, who knows? This question puzzles psychologists to this day. Regardless of whether we want to admit it, we all want to feel as if we are a little bit better than the people around us. We begin to establish that sense of superiority, some by exhibiting such behaviors as disdain or arrogance towards others. Others establish that sense of superiority in their own minds through the adornments of wealth, such as branded clothing, jewelry, luxury automobiles, and exclusive neighborhoods. Even amongst the poorest people, we find symbols that establish their status. When those status symbols are visible, and when they can be easily recognized, they can create the powerfully motivating emotion of *envy*.

Status symbols are objects that people use in order to signify their economic and social standards of living. Luxury items, large houses, expensive cars are all symbols that the upper class uses to define its position in social circles. A clear example is the newest trend of owning the latest version of mobile phones, such as the iPhone 5 or the Blackberry. These can become more of a status symbol then a device to use out of necessity.

However, most satisfaction acquired through attaining status symbols is short lived. Over time, such trappings become meaningless to us, at which point we seek genuine achievements to prove our worth. Research suggests that after reaching a certain income level an individual's happiness does not increase until he or she reaches the status of super-rich. Instead, as we grow wealthy, we become blasé or still want more, and again the vicious circle is in motion.

Nevertheless, status can continue to motivate us long after money ceases to do so. In today's world many people use the lure of status to motivate their employees; they bestow a new title with added responsibilities yet with no additional pay in order to reward their employees. All human beings can be motivated in a similar fashion. When I first started working at the university where I am today, I realized that when you march as a faculty member, there are different colors for people to wear depending on their earned degree, and you stand in line according to your years in the university. I found myself scanning fellow lecturers to note their statuses. Of course the doctoral position was the highest; that visual representation of real status has definitely been among my motivators to stay at the same university and try to finish my PhD.

In many countries around the world, status is attained through proper breeding. However, if we take the example of the United States in particular; the people who have power, influence and status there today have come from nowhere such as—to name only a few—Bill Gates, Oprah Winfrey, Warren Buffet, and the Bush family. This is by no means to say that in the United States status does not exist or that power there does not have its own merits. Of course it does, but in that part of the world status must be earned. People have a choice and they can also forge for themselves the life that they believe will give them fulfillment and move away from the life they were born into. However, there are others, like David Seagel, who achieved wealth by developing timeshare vacations through Westgate Resorts and made his newly found fortune. Amongst other vulgar behaviors, he decided to build the largest home he could, one with 30 bathrooms and 10 kitchens. When asked why he needed to build such a big house, he answered, "Because I could." A documentary, *The Queen of Versailles*, portrayed many of the behaviors of the "nouveau riche," though it also mirrors the behavior of many others. Seagel is a typical representation of the parvenus who exist today in all parts of the world and in some areas more than others, depending on each country's economic state of affairs. Some countries have strong economies in which sudden increases in wealth are uncommon, such as Denmark or Sweden, while some countries, such as Qatar and Saudi Arabia, have relatively new economies, and the discovery of natural resources has occasioned economic booms in which people rise to extreme wealth in no time.

Today many people believe that without achieving a certain status, they are incompetent members of society, but status doesn't always work to one's benefit. Some will be motivated to aspire for more and be motivated by people with status in positive ways, while others will use their socioeconomic status as a benchmark at which to remain in a negative way.

Having discussed status, attitudes toward money, and basic motivators, we need to examine the value system that gives rise to our own values. Values are instilled in us from childhood, and the three main factors that influence our values are family, school and society.

In my home, when I was little, my mother taught us that values are what make us strong, and that through them we can weather the winds. Family values are basically the rules or ideals that a family agrees to live by and stay true to. Each family has its own set of values unique to it. Tight-knit families are built on strong foundations of well-defined values. For each family member to be confident and trustworthy, he or she needs strong and consistent family values. What is of value in one family is not necessarily of value in another, or the hierarchy of importance of values may not be the same from one family to another. For example, in my family we value communication as a top value. Exchanging ideas and communicating our emotional state are very important considerations for us. Another family may not view things the same way; however, that family might value belonging or generosity as core values. Such differences by no means indicate that another family has lower self-esteem or fewer values than mine. That family is simply unique. Nevertheless, all families need to have a set of values.

Parents play the most significant role in their children's lives. All the values that people will live by, and through which they will develop strength, are built from childhood. Parents thus set the driving force of their children's future. They may not realize how greatly their words or actions influence their sons or daughters, or how deeply their actions impact their children's self worth. Unfortunately, children today are criticized, yelled at and punished far more than they are encouraged, loved or praised. Family time is short, and it is all too frequently spent explaining to the children what they have done wrong.

On the other side of the coin, many parents are extremely busy amassing their fortunes, so they end up spending very little time with their offspring. Then to compensate for their guilt and make up for lost time, they develop an inability to say "no" to their children's requests, as if they are trying to buy their children's love. Unfortunately, this strategy is not something that children tend to grow up to be grateful for. Once those children are adults themselves, they end up blaming their parents for not teaching them about the hardships of life and for making them feel that life is easy. Moreover, they are often aware that their system of values has been compromised. Their parents did not spend enough time with them to sew them in values.

Some of the Glamour Globals have been trying so hard to compete with the *old money* that their greed for money and power has led them to become more self-focused. Some go to the extent of ignoring the people around them as if they are insignificant, and of believing that what is allowed for them does not apply to others. Their children can be part of this detachment. Those characteristics, of detachment and disregard, are unfortunately values that can be ingrained in youngsters.

I don't want to sound as if I am bitterly suggesting that all people who have made their money anew will behave badly. There are exceptions who did do not fall into greed and believe in other human beings. The easiest example to point out would be Warren Buffett, who has pledged the majority of his money to charities.

CHAPTER THIRTEEN:
RAISING GLAMOUR GLOBALS

PARENTS ARE REPRIMANDING THEIR CHILDREN more than working on instilling in them a healthy self esteem. Self esteem is one of the cornerstones of developing a well-grounded individual who is able to think for him or herself and be a trendsetter rather than a follower. Self-esteem will give children, and thus future adults, the ability to feel good about themselves. Whether they develop this sort of healthy self regard or not will influence their decisions throughout their lives. Children, like everyone else, need to feel loved, appreciated and wanted.

As Yasmine, my co-author, said, let's start with basics. Children need to learn how to make decisions and age-appropriate choices and to deal with the responsibility of their choices. They need to know that consequences are a result of their own decisions and are not a mistake that everyone else is making, and not they themselves.

Children's role models are their parents in the majority of cases. Given a lack of quality time with parents and few shared experiences with them, children tend to have weak knowledge of what behaviors are appropriate, as well as what behaviors should and should not be modeled. This deficit alone is enough to explain why children may be inclined to become superficial—to become Glamour Globals; it is easier to follow behaviors than to work through the problems posed by values and morals.

Discipline creates boundaries for children, and these boundaries allow the child to be contained and to cultivate higher self-esteem.

Parents should set limits on their children's behavior and on how they speak to others. These rules and limits will protect children emotionally and physically and thus give them a sense of control over their lives. Limits will make them more confident in their choices and will help them become better consumers.

I still remember when my five-year-old daughter came home and posed a spontaneous yet serious question about why another member of our family had a much bigger house and a huge pool. She seemed truly upset upon this realization. I did want her to take pride in what her father and I were providing for her and in all our other accomplishments. It was a great opportunity for me to instill pride in her for what she already had but took for granted. One mistake that so many parents make is to start comparing their lives with those of people who are less fortunate. In the child's mind it is like, "Why is she comparing me to those people?" I remember telling my daughter about all our assets in terms of love and a happy home, describing her bedroom that contains most of the things she has collected and explaining the things she truly needs. This approach, I think, prompted her to think for herself and see whether anything important was truly missing from her life. I also explained to her a basic truth of life: not everyone who works earns the same income. People are different. Since that time I don't recall hearing her compare herself to anyone else. Today she is eleven and has become the spokesperson when my two younger daughters become inquisitive about the material aspects of other peoples' lives.

Another issue that our future buyers in the making are experiencing is a lack of stability in their households. There are various reasons for this instability. We are seeing many divorces, which can make children less emotionally stable if not all aspects of the divorce are addressed. Children of divorce may feel their lives are a failure and thus tend to have low self-esteem. They may become introverted and easily influenced. Children who come from a home that sees several partner changes, or in which there are issues of abuse and/or parents who do not have permanent jobs are more likely to face instability in their own lives later. These children can become more fragile and develop negative self-talk that eventually causes depression and anxiety. They find themselves in a vicious circle—they may very well try as adults to find a sense of worth or release their anxiety by concentrating on material things, because these, as empty of content as they are, nonetheless do not let you down or hurt you. Recent research has emphasized the great extent to which children's overall happiness, independence, and success depends on parents building healthy self esteem in their children and teens. Growing up is a long journey and a difficult one, but it can lead to success when backed up with a good positive support system. The people that are constant in our lives throughout our developing years will have an impact on who we become as adults.

How teenagers are modeled into buyers

As I mentioned above, parental influence has a strong impact on the development of morals and values. When these are not instilled from childhood, teenagers become more restless and more easily influenced. Teenagers will follow in the footsteps of their parents in their buying habits and the justifications of their desires regardless of their actual needs.

Parents are not the only ones to influence teens. A wide range of media personalities now impact the lives of teenagers. Teens do have positive role models such as Oprah and Angelina Jolie, who through their many organizations have motivated youth to do more charity and community work. Unfortunately, however, not all teens are motivated by such well-rooted causes, but instead love to follow the Kardashians and other celebrities leading the latest trends. These teens are not taught to select important information or detect relevant messages from celebrity watching, but instead enjoy the imaginary intimacy they develop with those personalities. They know all the little details of these celebrities' lives, including their most intimate thoughts, and they often end up modeling those celebrities' behaviors. Human nature made us curious, and we might all enjoy a little bit of "voyeurism," but these reality shows have taken people-watching to another, potentially harmful, level.

Teenagers are major trendsetters; we need only to look at the case of Justin Bieber, and observe how many purple items were sold in the last two years…

Celebrities have influenced teens and adults alike from the days of the very first silent movies. However, the time spent in those entertainments was formerly much more limited. Today media consumption has become a culture of its own, and the culture indirectly pressures people to be followers. A great example would be the upward shift in the prevalence of eating disorders and the downward shift in the age of their onset. Today it is not uncommon to hear of a girl of eight who suffers from anorexia. The media has encouraged models and actresses to promote the sort of unhealthy body image that spurs on these disorders.

The music industry also influences our teens' perspective. The words of song lyrics and the images from videos portray the latest gadgets and trends, and these have become huge motivators in what we would like to be or identify ourselves with.

One of the major influences on our decisions to feel that we are trendy and are fitting into the bigger picture is the media; it guides our buying habits or opinions concerning the right neighborhood to live in, the right size of house to own, the right car to drive, or even the shoe brand we should choose. This influence becomes the subculture's identity; we are not after quality so much as a sense of belonging. Our defenses are down when we are watching any form of entertainment. Subliminal messages are introduced through movies or advertisements, and we unconsciously register these messages.

Last but not least, we must consider the powerful influence of peer pressure. We are all social animals by default, and we all want to belong. Thus, we choose friends who we believe identify us as they represent the elite group in our perception. Some of us are strong and stand our ground, while others give in and follow trends. Which path matters will take goes back to the children's confidence and self esteem and the way they have been taught to think for themselves and believe in their actions.

Chapter Fourteen:
The Impact

WHILE I WAS LIVING IN London, I had a friend who was extremely smart and a high achiever. A few years later we bumped into each other again, and I was surprised to notice that all she wanted to talk about was the latest Leboutin shoes, the latest trends in clothing, where she travelled and what hotels she stayed at. And while she was talking, I couldn't help but wonder where the highly intelligent, hard-working high achiever friend I knew had gone. What had changed her? Why was she enjoying spending two hours talking about frivolous topics even though we hadn't seen each other in a while? What had caused this change? Please don't misunderstand me; I love to talk about the latest trends and so forth, but I do not enjoy doing so for two hours with a friend whom I haven't seen in a long time. She was behaving like a typical Glamour Global—giving herself importance by naming brands or being frivolous to sound cooler. I mean we have to admit very serious and smart people are sometimes boring, not cool! Cool is the image supplied by the various sources of knowledge we have today. Because of my job, I am curious about human nature and what can make us change so drastically.

Today we face a trend of people not being loyal to any brand; even physicians are not loyal to pharmaceutical companies, a departure which is costing those companies a lot of money. Why are we less loyal today? What is causing us to be trend followers rather than trend makers? Meanwhile, we seem ever more capable of condescending to our fellows and flashing our possessions, of building our egos based on the demeaning of others around us—why?

The main factors that play a substantial role in consumers' buying behaviors are the attacks on our decision-making from the media and the social values people follow today. The lack of a pressing need, which is usually the core motivation creating a sense of urgency for something, has been compromised by our lack of confidence and the pressures that society places on individuals to be valued based on their possessions rather than based on their achievements, beliefs and integrity.

Our perceptions of what is meaningful and what is a need compared to our wants and desires have become blurred. This blurring is the result, among other things, of all the "bling bling" we are constantly exposed to in the media. Quality is not marketed; rather, what is marketed is the perceived necessity of following in the footsteps of those with higher social status and completely different demographics, regardless of whether the things being marketed fit our beliefs, values or culture. The positive things we may have learned are being unlearned because being trendy and associated with the right crowd or belonging to the elite group pays off better, giving individuals an illusion of belongingness. Thus, the old principles and morals we might have learned before are slipping, because society tends not to repay these standards. Thus, we are seeing a decline in principles as well. Beliefs and attitudes are typically difficult to change, given that they stem from an early lifestyle and an individual's personality. But in today's world individuals are starting to realize the positive consequences of their behaviors when they imitate the elite groups or the people with "bling bling," and thus the information is being distorted and beliefs and attitudes are compromised to make them consistent with what they think they need.

I have come to the realization that we all want to be socially accepted so badly that we can lose track of what "stuff" means to us or what values we hold. Moreover, today, with all our new technologies and industrial development, we are becoming capricious and blasé, while the glamorous world is at everyone's fingertips. Marketing strategists are betting on this lapse in our judgment, and are luring people to become involved in the lives of celebrities until they start identifying with them and thus become eager to have the possessions of these celebrities, such as what Victoria Beckham or Beyoncé has been wearing, regardless of the consumer's need for or ability to afford those goods. Some people go so far as to put their names on waiting lists at the mall or even search the continent to find the right pair of jeans.

Ads are working on creating an emotional bond with consumers, but because of all the studies of buying behaviors and triggers, we are being bombarded with too many options, and we human beings are easily confused by such variety and masses of choice. Moreover, competition is very high, so customers are losing their focus and loyalty. This situation finds individual tastes shifting rapidly in lieu of building a relationship with brands.

Appearances are becoming everything; I have the biggest house, you have the best car, she has the best collection of signee pants. These are all expressions we hear today, whereas not long ago it was considered bad upbringing if we spoke about such materialistic matters. Today we have come under such pressure from friends and society that we are making poor judgments and irrational decisions. Marketing agencies have realized that individuals today are shopping for an excess of ownership rather than for value or need.

Human beings are trustful by nature; otherwise, we wouldn't be able to achieve anything. We love flattery and have some vanity in us. The media has learned well how to play on these traits, turning us into puppets that follow trends and brands that are succeeding regardless of our need, or the company's integrity or transparency in selling. Building loyal consumers has become immensely challenging in our world today. Meanwhile, the speed of the development of technology has created a futile need in the individual for constant competition and has become paralleled with the emergence of more and more individuals with superficial wants and a desperate need to be accepted socially. Unfortunately all this striving has come to a destructive synergy. I don't want to deny the importance of technology and how it helped us move forward in most aspects of our lives. But if we take the example of Apple, specifically the development of the iPhone, we realize what puppets we are becoming. We buy a phone that is quite expensive, thinking we have bought something very special, and three months later they come up with a newer version with very few changes and our device suddenly becomes old. It's a constant struggle to keep up that has nothing to do with what we need apart from being able to have the latest gadget and for people to see us as trendy.

Having discussed the influence of family, friends and the media on our psychological makeup as consumers we need to determine the most necessary basic principles we need to instill in our children.

Building an emotionally stronger individual can forestall all these dire trends as we encourage children not to seek to follow others, especially when doing so means giving up some of their principles, and even when being their own person contradicts their eagerness to be considered "cool." Strong self esteem will create less impulsive buyers.

The culture we are born into and the perceptions of the larger society will influence our perception of right and wrong, and of what is acceptable. We have to realize that we cannot give ourselves value through material things. There is no value in buying anything. We do not need to shop to exist. The constant desire to be liked by others will weaken us. The belief that our worthiness of attention or time and our ability to be accepted come from products, and that these products will make us worthy or acceptable, will always make us followers rather than trend-setters. In the end, however, behaviors can be changed. More importantly, individuals can change their behaviors.

It must be said that any improvement in the deeply ingrained patterns my co-authors and I have described in this book must be incremental and gradual, at least at first. But in a way, that's great news: Incremental and gradual change is exactly the sort of change it is possible for all of us to make! In other words, the only kind of change we can make is well within our reach. If we do so, then I believe eventually, the history of cultural improvements shows us, when enough incremental change trends in the right direction, we may reach a tipping point, and the incremental change will become a revolution. At that point, we will be able to look at Glamour Global behavior primarily as an oddity of the history of our development, perhaps as an occasional anomaly of our present. But most importantly, we will find that Glamour Globals no longer have the power to define the culture. That task, of declaring who we are, will then be left to the better angels of our nature.

EPILOGUE:
SAID BAAGHIL

M Y INTEREST IN THE GLAMOUR Globals, as I have shared previously, first emerged because I care about brands, and because I have observed over the years how the Glamour Global phenomenon poses a challenge and even a threat to my work in brand cultivation and maintenance. Because of Glamour Globalism, a great deal of purchasing power and a great deal of potential to move the market forward in sensible directions, it seems to me, is now being largely wasted. But because my interest in the Glamour Globals emerged based on my passion for brands, I think it now bears mentioning, as we close, why I care so much about brands.

Anyone who has read my other books knows that for me, a brand is far more than merely a logo or an advertising scheme. Brands are about relationships—deeper connections between companies and their customers. Brands imply a way of doing business in which companies design their product lines after listening to what customers need, and then cultivate customer loyalty by sharing the story of the company. If the exchange is successful, consumers find their real needs met, and companies find that they have become a part of their customers' lives.

In short, my vision of why brands are important is that they're about people. Brands place humanity in its rightful place at the center of commercial exchanges, and bring some warmth and meaning to what would otherwise be a merely crass transaction for gain. While the need for status may indeed be a human need, and it may therefore be a real need of consumers, it's one of the few needs that comes purely at the expense of other people: I can gain in status only by surpassing someone else's status. Where many aspects of business, including marketing, are now moving in the direction of aiming for a win–win, the pathologically based buying habits of the Glamour Globals, by definition, aim for "I win, you lose."

The Glamour Globals thus pose a threat not only to brands, but to certain fabrics of value that society depends on to bring meaning and happiness to life—valuing others, building relationships, seeing the big picture, among others. We could also say it another way: The various kinds of damage Glamour Globals do to societal values pose a threat to brands.

In general, I have observed, contemporary practices in branding and marketing are grounded in certain kinds of economic maturity, and those practices can therefore get out of kilter pretty quickly when they encounter instances of gross economic immaturity. The sort of crass materialism that follows trends instead of being open to brand relationships can be thought of as a sort of consumer juvenile delinquency—driven by immediate gratification and an impulse to fit in and rise, with little to no thought for longer term consequences or deeper sources of value.

I sought the help of my co-authors in this inquiry for many reasons—but two very important motivations bear mentioning here. In the first place, the Glamour Global phenomenon touches so many areas of contemporary life in the developing world that any book that seeks to size up the Glamour Globals as a group could scarcely succeed without taking a number of looks at the situation, from a variety of perspectives. In a related vein, I knew at the outset that my feelings on the subject were so strong that I would do well to double-check my reactions against those of some other thoughtful writers. In a variety of ways, I am convinced this book would have had far less to offer had it not been for the remarkable contributions of Miriam, Rola, and Yasmine.

In the second place, given that I'm asking people to let go of the quest for status in deference to deeper values, I thought this might be an excellent time to try de-centering myself a bit as the author, to share some status, and to thus perhaps offer an example of how we can move things forward through fostering collaboration and relationship. I thought it would be interesting and useful to take a slightly more democratic approach to authorship than we often find in the business world.

In that regard, I have been deeply gratified. The experience of sharing the authorship of this book has been a wonderful affirmation for me of how much there is to gain by opening up discussions to new voices. My co-authors have my gratitude not only for their work with pen and keyboard, but for teaching me anew the value of making room for new voices, through the vivid example of their excellent contributions.

The book that has emerged from this collaboration has given me a lot to think about. Such could scarcely have been the result, I think it's safe to say, if I had been the book's sole author. But I hope and trust that the book has given us all some things to think about. I am obviously passionate about what I see as the negative impact of the Glamour Globals on markets and brands. I hope, however, that my passion will not be mistaken for bitterness or ill will. There is something for all of us in the lessons that we've suggested here are needful for the Glamour Globals. I imagine there is scarcely a human being whose palms have been crossed by cash who hasn't struggled with the green demon of status acquisition and its twin, the red imp of low self esteem. Perhaps one of the reasons I'm passionate on the subject of Glamour Globals is that I see in their behavior a battleground for some struggles that I have been through myself.

However that may be, I'm pleased to see—in part as this book's author, and in part as its reader—that the volume that has emerged not only takes an unflinching look at its subject, but is also filled with compassion for that subject. Along the way the book surprised me in striking some quite hopeful strains.

I remain a believer in the developing world, both its people and its markets, and in its potential to bring value to the world even in the act of addressing its own challenges. I hope that this book will similarly inspire readers. Each of the problems we've identified here is paired with a possibility. For myself—as a marketing professional, a writer and a student of people—I find myself closing the experience of producing this book with a renewed sense of all the great things that remain possible for the people of emerging economies.